Petals of a Flower

Catriona Noone

ISBN (Print Edition): 978-1-54395-362-6

ISBN (eBook Edition): 978-1-54395-363-3

petals
of a
flower

CATRIONA NOONE

I would like to dedicate this book to my nephew Garron, who was a great help to me in getting this on track, I'm very proud of him, I also have a poem for him in the book called Light in My Day x

YOU KNOW

You know within your own heart
What you must do
You know you're the only one
Who can make your dreams come true?
You know you're the only one
That knows the real you
You know you can be the tallest tree
If you get the morning dew
You know you're like a silk thread
Delicate but strong
You know you're like a sheaf of barley
And you'll catch the morning sun
You know you are a little star
That hides behind them all
You know someday you'll know
How to break your fall
You know a day will come
When you'll realise what you need
You know that the most beautiful flower
Came from a humble seed

WONDER

Did you ever wonder why the fields are green?
Did you ever wonder why it's a silent scream?

Did you ever wonder why the sky is blue?
Did you ever wonder why I stopped loving you?

Did you ever wonder how a seed becomes a flower?
Did you ever wonder at a warm April shower?

Did you ever wonder why the birds can fly?
Did you ever wonder and say, why can't?

Did you ever wonder about the nature of a storm?
Did you ever wonder why it leaves things beaten and torn?

Did you ever wonder at the simplicity of life?
Did ever wonder why it cuts like a knife?

Did you ever wonder just to pass the time?
Did you ever wonder if your imaginations lying?

WINTER

The darkened day of winters song
The bleak, the dark the chill of dawn
The frost that formed the crystal clear
The life that froze a tiny tear
The storm that raged on and on
The delivery of destruction greets the dawn
The landscape changed from old to new
A chance perhaps to change the view
The snow that covers all it sees
The balancing act it does with ease
The life that's hiding deep inside
The hidden world that brims with life
The scene that we no longer see
The eye that catches what it wants it to be
The spring will come to release all life
The chapter changes from dark to light
The winters story to recharge and rest
The perfect season to start the next

WHEN YOU

When you smile I want to share your happiness
When you hurt I want to ease your pain, so you can feel again
When you listen, I want to be your ears to hear what you hear
When you see I want to be your eyes to share your vision
When you are free I want to be the wings that take you to your future
When you are in the dark I want to be the one who takes you to the light
So you don't have to fight
When you are released to smell the roses I want to be the one who grows
them for you
When your heart beats I want to be the rhythm that you feel
When you walk your road I want to be the direction that you seek

WHEN I FEEL...

When I feel time goes slow
Then I feel I don't know
When I feel hope is gone
Then I know I must be strong
When I feel I'm in fire inside?
Then I know I have too much pride
When I feel I'm a leaf in the wind
Then I know I must defend
When I feel I'm washed out
Then I know that I'm a cloud
When I feel I want to fly
Then I know for you I must try
When I feel I want to follow the sun
Then I know I'm the untamed one
When I feel you were wrong
Then I know I must carry on
When I feel that I am free
Then I know it must be me

WATER

I reflect the sun the moon and the stars
I'm the air we breathe
I am intoxicating
I am a fountain of youth
A reservoir for the world
You kill me
You pollute me
You mess with my cycle
You're bleeding me dry
And all my creativeness
And so, in turn I come back to you
But not knowingly poison you slowly
You don't care for me as I've cared for you
You don't respect me
You don't understand my power
But someday you will
I just hope it's not too late.........
For both of us

VALENTINE

I am yours as you are mine
I'm glad you are my valentine
I searched the stars just for you
That's when I saw you smiling at me too
As you placed your hand in mine
I knew we'd be together 'till the end of time
True loves truth, a gentle kiss
Our hearts and souls in total bliss
My valentine, my rose my bud
A forever bloom that is our love

ME

I may not fit in but that's just me
I may not like reality, but I like my dreams
I may not like you, you may not like me
This is my story, so I can do what I please
I may not like the weather but then maybe I do
I may not be beautiful, but my charm will get me through
I may not be right but I'm definitely not wrong
I may not be old because I'm forever young
I may be talking crap that's easy to do
Have a laugh at yourself and you won't feel so blue
If there was a corner in a circle that's where I'd be
I'm an unusual shape
I'm only as perfect as I can be

UNDER COVER

Hidden voices from within
Screaming out their voices grim
Under the cover of dark they dwell
The noise inside cannot be quelled
Flows like lava burning hot
As it goes it turns to rock
The molten lava will continue to grow
An island of black beneath the rose
The petals fall but nothing grows
So, nothing ever hears its woes

UNCLEAR

Your tears are like snow drops
Falling from the sky
Falling from your face
For an emotional goodbye
So bitter yet so sweet
So clear yet so unclear
A half story to be told
The other half disappears
The pleasure and the pain
Which one will win out
Will we be summer in the winter?
Or a desert in a drought

TRAPPED

Running through the night
Dashing out of sight
To a world of isolation

Fear sits in the corner
With nowhere to run
Gets nothing done

A disfigured figure
That can't walk talk
Lack of communication

Defences built high
Not visible to the naked eye
An invisible wall stands tall

Can I show you my world?
Can I let you come inside?

Or is it too hard to try......

TOGETHER

A silky film of thread
Takes off and starts to fly
Carried by the breeze
Through the countryside
Meets more along the way
And then they all hold hands
With unity together
There's nothing they can't withstand
If we were like those threads
Blowing in the breeze
Could we bond together
To form a blanket of peace

THE TIDES OF TIME

The tides of time
Are flowing in rhyme
They ebb and flow
In their own rushed rows

Erosion of emotions
Being washed away
Washed by the water
Into the bay

What's left on the rocks
Is only debris
Of another washed up life
If it's not me

Back on the sand
Another life stands
Staring it down
Waiting for good times to come around

Stares a familiar face
With the tears of a stranger

THE ONE

You're the one who always had my heart
You're the one who let me be and set me free
You're the one who made my heart complete and it's never missed a beat
You're the one who made my blood flow and never let go
You're the one who took me by surprise when I looked into your eyes
You're the one who taught me how to speak so I don't feel so weak
You're the one who saved me from the storm and made me feel warm
You're the one that is my drug of choice and the only one that I'll ever need
You're the one who I would walk the earth for, so we could walk together
You're the one who showed me how to love and be loved
You're the one who I will never let go because you make me feel so...........

THE JOURNEY

To all that is mythical
To all that is real
To all your heart can give
To all your heart can steal
To all that you can follow
To all that follow through
To all that live the dream
To all that never do
To all that makes you laugh
To all that makes you crawl
To all that makes you diverse
To all that makes you your all
To all that life throws at you
To all that you throw back
To all that you can see
To all that fades to black
To all that shines before you
To all that pulls you through
To all that you can touch
To all that reach out and touch you
To all there is a lesson from the things we do
To all that are on a journey
may the best of luck come to you

SUNSHINE

You're like a little ray of light
A shimmer in the sun
The smile upon your face
Can catch the untamed one
It captured me and brought me to tears
Brought me to where the clouds disappeared
I could now see
That you were the one
My little ray of sunshine
My flower in the sun

STAY STRONG

Did you ever have a time when everything felt sad?
But everything you needed was everything you had
Way deep down inside where it hurt to feel
Where somewhere in this life you were there for real
You go through many things you never let you cry
You never let you give up you must try
So, you muddle through this life for so long
Somehow in the end the weak had made you strong
You didn't recognise it 'till you came out into the sun
Now when you look around that big old cloud is gone

SPIRIT

Run wild run free
Your spirit; let it be
Gentle breeze goes through the trees
And bring my spirit with gentle ease

Past the woods into the dawn
Let it rise with the sun
Let it go from east to west
At sunset let it rest

Let it swim let it fly
Let it find the reason why
Let it live don't let it die
Please don't make it cry

Let it smile let it have fun
May it never be undone
Let it learn to live a life
Without trouble or any strife

Let it learn let it feel
Let it love itself for real
Let it take me and I'll follow
Let it never end in sorrow

My spirit is me my spirit is free!

SPELLBOUND

The magic that comes from within
And its world begins to spin
The mystery inside is most profound
Dark and deep underground
The leather-bound books
The spells inside
And the world it wants to hide
The elusive lock the secret key
The door to this world not for me
From page to page deadly curses
Are awaiting those happy verses
The spell is spun the web is strong
Here comes the awakening with the dawn
The dawn is dusk the day is night
The sun the moon the stars shine bright
The magic builds the mystery inside
The clock struck twelve it's time to hide

SILENT FEAR

Meandering wandering lost and found
Into the abyss and under ground
Over the grass and under the trees
Life is sailing in the breeze
From me to you to them to all
Can we hear natures call?
when we listen, what do we hear
Perhaps it's a silent fear
A black tulip begins to weep
In its own silent sleep
It ripples out along the way
It's calls getting tired day after day
If I help you will you help me too
Please hold my hand and walk me through
From angles to demons we have them all
They are part of our wings and part of our fall
A silent eagle watches on
With his furrowed brow he can see
What we are what we should be

SHADOWS

Shadows on the water
Are slowly washed away
Shadows from the moonlight
Fade from night to day
Shadows in the corner
Hide the pain away
Shadows from the trees give a dappled shade
Shadows from the sun
Tell the length of the day
Shadows from the strange
Turn into something new
Shadows from our lives
Take over me and you
Shadows from the flame
That come from the fire
Shadows on the heart
Are the shadows I desire

SEARCH YOUR SOUL FOR ANSWERS

Search your soul for answers
For it's the truth that you must find
What you want from your life
What you need defined

Search your soul for answers
Do you like what you see
Is it the way you thought it would be?
Will it set you free?

Search your soul for answers
For within your soul you lie
Search your soul for answers
Does it make you want to cry?

Search your soul for answers
Are they hidden deep
Does it hide from this world?
The secrets you wish to keep

Search your soul for answers
Are you afraid being you
What's so wrong with who you are
To your self be true

Search your soul for answers
And it will give you peace
The peace of mind to sleep at night
And not be afraid to dream..........

RISE ABOVE

You will be gone, and I will be strong
You left me so much pain, but I will rise again
From the ashes I will grow
Like a flower in the snow
Like white water in a river
Eventually it will simmer
Though the time may feel slow
I'm pushing forward as I go
Like the sun behind the clouds
I will not be covered behind a shroud
Like the quarter moon
I will eventually reach full bloom
When I search among the stars
I'll be the brightest one of all by far

R.I.P. CHESTER BENNINGTON

Our hearts they hurt for you so
Just one more breath before you go
Before life extinguishes your sweet glow
The last tear cried the forever song
The light that takes you to your dawn
Out of the darkness you will fly
And wait for you to say goodbye
I can't imagine, and I wonder why
Why life's direction took you to the sky
But you are free you hurt no more
Life has both shut and opened a door

READY

Are you ready for the dawn?
For a light that's not yet shone
When it wakes you will see?
A light so bright a path so free

I'll follow in your shadow
As you lead me away
To a land where make believe
is real everyday

now the sun shines before you
and the shadow that you make
stretches out before me
from morning till the end of day

A fantasy that's real
Even though it's fake
The ripples of your life
Reflected on the lake

The brightness of the moon
The biggest star of all
Bursts through the sky
To light the stars that never fall

So whether it's light from the day
Or from the night
A dreamers dream
Will take off
With its own special light

POWER WITHIN

The tears that fall
The nights that crawl
The darkness within
The secret sin
The act before you
Leaves you blind
The frightening forecast
The wicked mind
The power within
The truth it would ignite
The magic spark
The flame that wouldn't die

POTENTIAL

Fishing from the moon
Catch a falling star
Reaching for a dream
They all seem too far
Have I pushed them all away?
Where have they all gone
Are they still in my head buried deep inside
To breathe life into them
And make them come alive
To remind me who I was
To who I can be
I am my own potential
I am the power within me

PETALS OF A FLOWER

Petals of a flower, a blanket of snow
Ashes that fall when its's time to let go
The fruit has fallen, the raindrops grow
Does anyone hear the tree that falls?
Perhaps the forest around it that hears its call
The fallen leaves in autumn song
The feathers in the wind see-saw on and on
The frost that preserves everything it sees
The rays of the sun ready to tease

PERHAPS

Perhaps I wonder all the time
Perhaps I wonder if your mine
Perhaps I don't belong to you
Perhaps you'll have to live with that too
Perhaps I wonder about many things
Perhaps I'm going round in rings
Perhaps your right, perhaps you're wrong
Perhaps I'm God and I'll live on
Perhaps I don't know what to do
Perhaps perchance I'm just like you
Perhaps I don't know when to stop
Perhaps I'm running 'till I drop
Perhaps I don't have much to say
Perhaps you'll have to accept me this way
Perhaps maybe sometime so what
Perhaps I'm normal perhaps I'm not

PERFECT

A gentle soul
A little bug
The softest fleece
The fluffiest rug
The kindest heart
Made from desire
The bird that sings
take me higher
the little child
so innocent within
in this world
there should be no sin
as strong as a web
that holds your dream
and holds it for you
until you come calling
the whitewashed stone
the flurry of snow
the perfect dream
the perfect flow
the person within
the beautiful ghost
the angel calling
the perfect toast

PAST/PRESENT

When the time is right you'll see the light
You won't have to fight not tonight
The light will make its way down a long dark road
Showing the new stuff as well as the old
Because with some of the old and some of the new
You'll see where to change your attitude to get a better view
For a better view is what you must find
It won't change the past but can help leave it behind
Leave it behind is what you must do
So, you can change your life to make a better you
When you make a better you, you will find
A better life though it may not always be kind
So, come as you are not as you were
Because there's no future in the past and no past in the future
So it's up to you what you want to do

OCEAN

I am the ocean
That tares at my heart
I am the ocean
That takes us further apart
I am the ocean sometimes
Choppy sometimes calm
I am the ocean
To the depths I am
I am the ocean
Lapping gently to the shore
I am the ocean
Sent to engulf you once more
I am the ocean
Time to take on something new
I am the ocean
Please don't poison me too

NOW WE ARE FREE

Now we are free
Together we will be
Through the doors to elysian
To eternity

Now we are free
To slip away
Together hand in hand
Together all the way

Now we are free
We've found a way
Loves young dream
Let it never fade away

Now we are free
It was time to escape
Our fears from this world
And it to be ok

Now we are free
to blow in the breeze
the same; but different
And somehow at ease

Now we are free
As deep as the ocean
As we stand on the shore
Our lives are in motion

NATURE

It's always coldest near the dawn
It's always warmest near the sun
It always sparkles with the stars
To the heavens and onto mars
It always glows with the moon
Morning always comes too soon
It's always rough with winters breeze
In the summer it blows with ease
It's always refreshing in the spring
And the water begins to sing
It gurgles on into the summer
One of nature's little plumbers

NATURE AT ITS BEST

The perfect flower yellow gold
Nestled into the moss forever it will grow
It rests its little head upon the moss-covered rock
For the sun to shine upon it so it can shine back
Every year it will return nature at its best
It doesn't ask for anything it lives wild and free
Lucky I am to be in its presence smiling up at me

MYSTERIOUS

I live in hope I live in fear
I live in wonder that you're here
Who are you from where did you come
Did you rise with the morning sun?
Are you a butterfly with painted wings
Or a flower in the sun that begins to sing
A ladybird perhaps or even a bee
That bumbles along wild and free
Or a dew coated web in the shape of a heart
That I couldn't resist right from the start

MORE

What it took to get here
There is no turning back
What it took to get here
When everything was black
What it took to get here
To get out of your own way
What it took to get here
To pray from night to day
What it took to get here
Where did the light come from?
What it took to get here
To rise with the morning sun
What it took to get here
The reasons are many more
What it took to get here
To open lives door
What it took to get here
I will go and more

MAYBE

Maybe people aren't all the same
Maybe they're not all the blame
Maybe there are some out there like me
Maybe they are also free

Maybe we are meant to be; something out there wild and free
Maybe we are like the stars; each our own yet so far
Maybe we are like the sun; burning bright yet still undone
Maybe we are like the moon; so far away yet so soon

Maybe we are all creative; each one our own native
Maybe we are all so strong; fighting hard and moving on
Maybe we are at one with nature; maybe it's our creator
Maybe we are the birds in the sky; each on a different high

Maybe we're forever young; but our mask carries on

Maybe, maybe, maybe what?
Maybe don't know, maybe not

MADMAN

The madman cries
Under evil eyes
Through the burning skies
As he lies

The hours have passed
The ones that were supposed to last
Now they have been buried in sin

Darkness falls
The madman crawls
Looking for his mind
In a world he cannot find

His life to overcome
To a picture that looks dumb
For one who has begun
To stop being on the run

The madman cries
In a world he does despise
When he cannot end
He feels he can't depend......

LOVE

Even in the dark I can see your smile
Come with me and lets sit for a while
Cast away those shadows cast away the pain
Come into the light where we can see again
Will our loving memory be as real as it should be?
Swimming through the currents till they set us free
Till our lives are fluid and as happy as a flea
Through the ages of time until we get what's yours and mine
Because in the dark we are the light
We are a star that's shining bright
Through every day and every night
Love is love right is right

LONESTAR

This Lonestar wanders on along through the night
Followed by its shadow nothing else in sight
It's a shooting star but it's beginning to fall
Where will it land will it end it all

Does it have a demise does anybody know?
Maybe I'll just follow it see where it goes
Will it find a different world of its very own?
Will it take me with it or will we just wander on?

I am like that Lonestar in my own special way
Drifting along to a world that no one knows
To a world where you can't stay

LIGHT IN MY DAY

I saw a little light today but now he's far away
So very sharp and alert so very cute and small
So innocent to the world so unafraid of it all
Those eyes going through me wondering who's there
Still all the same didn't seem to care
That lights got a place in my heart always will be there
He brought joy to the world joy to all who cared
He's like a flicker in the night to those who look his way
He's new life to the world and he's here to stay
I saw a little light today but now he's far away
That's okay because he shines anyway
My little light is shining

LIFE

The burning rose that's nature's sun
The poppy fields that stretch on and on
The towering trees that watch over us all
Nature's bodyguards to protect us all
Meandering rivers from the mountains they rise
To the sun kissed plains all hold life
Without these things we cannot be
Here on this earth as human beings

I'LL BE THERE

Whenever you're feeling bad
Whenever you're feeling sad
Whenever you feel alone
Please know your home

Whenever you're feeling old
Whenever you're feeling cold
Whenever you feel your emotions gone
Please know for you my fires still on

Whenever you're feeling insane
Whenever you're feeling the blame
Whenever you feel it's not for real
Please know for you my heart would steal

Whenever you're feeling you can't fight the flow
Whenever you're feeling you just don't know
Whenever you feel your powers gone
Please know for you I will live on

I'D LOVE....

I'd Love if that were true?
That you would watch my dust
I'd love if that were true?
That I could be in lust
I'd love if that were true?
That I was as good as you
I'd love if that were true?
That you were as good as me too
I'd love if that were true?
That I am not critical
I'd love if that were true?
That I am perfect
I'd love if that were true?
That I was divine
I'd love if that were true?
But I may be lying

I LOVE WHEN

I love when the wind whistles outside
Because it stirs something within us
Like a flurry of leaves in an autumn breeze

I love when the sun shines on a summers day
Because it brightens up our lives
Like a ray of light showing the way

I love when the water ebbs and flows
Because it reminds us of our emotions
Like a trickle of water eventually creating a waterfall

I love when it's calm
Because it shrouds us with tranquillity
Like the sprinkling of snow that hugs everything it touches

I love when the moon and the stars shine as one
Because it reminds me of our potential for unity
Like us and our connection with nature

I love when a seed becomes a flower
Because it reminds us of how we came into being
Like the dispersing of different seeds that created the world

I love when we form a bond with someone
Because they make us feel forever young
Finally, your life has its own song
And together your hearts beat to the same drum

I AM

I am a bird with a broken wing
I am a bee without a sting
I am a flower that has no sun
I am alive the broken one
I am winter without a storm
I am a mirror but reflect no one
I am a colour black no white
I am the dark without the light
I am summer without the glow
I am the raindrop that turns to woe
I am a fire without a flame
I am me come alive again

ME

I am me, I am free
I am as happy as I could be
I am bold, I am brass
I am a wonder and I've got class
I am bright, I am dark
I am fire and I've got my own spark
I am wind, I am rain
I am a storm that will blow you away
I am the moon, I am the sun
I am the one who will change at dawn
I am the frost, I am the snow
I am the white wash over the stone
I am the one, who will carry you through
I am myself just for you

HOPE

Through every little breath
Comes every little storm
Through every little dusk
Comes every little dawn

Through every little heart
Comes a living beat
Through every little feeling
That brings you to your knees

Through every little flicker
Comes every little flame
Through every little raindrop
Comes a river again

Through every little tear
Comes a little smile
Through every little laugh
That wins by a mile

Through every little star
Comes a little dream
Through every little scar
Comes every little scream

Through every little passage
Comes a little journey
Through every little lesson
Laid out before me

Through every little song
Comes a different story
Every bit of strength
Carries it for me

HELP

Twisted slowly
Tossing hold me
Feeling mould me
Nothing controls me

Life that shows me
Dreams that warn me
Reality that throws me
Illusions that console me

Friends to trust?
Enemies haunt me
Strangers in my way
People confuse me

Words to explain
Talk to kill the pain
Like a seed of grain
You begin again!

HAWKEYES

As old Hawkeye died
He flew into the sky
To wave goodbye
In the vast landscape of rivers and rolling hills
His words echoed through the ages of time
Until they began to rhyme
For he was truly at one with nature
Because it was what kept him alive
He learned to fish and hunt
And in return gained the true wisdom of the land
He worked with it not against it
He kept it true for future generations
Until the white man came and destroyed the land
With so called progress
As hawk eyes looked down
He saw his land one of beauty
Being torn apart and all that would follow
Was destruction greed and egotism
A very different world from the one he knew
With little regard for animal and human alike
His wisdom lost but his truth remained

HAUNTING

She's black, she's bleak she's beautiful inside
Inside her dark and haunting eyes
Rivers of lava mixed with gold
Burning hot it cracks the mould
Through the split part of her seeped out
Spent a lifetime searching for the girl in the clouds
The black angel rises within her soul
Takes her to a river so cold
She can't breathe she can't give in
She's scared to think of what lies within
Her dark shadow has a shadow of its own
It's bleak too with a story to be told

HAPPY

A lonely little cloud
Floats across the sky
Into the great expanse
While the world watches by
Just floating along singing a song
Being as authentic as he can be
In his vast world his perfect world
His imagination is set free
What will he find on his journey
Maybe the sun and a gentle breeze
He lives his life happy out
Smiling down on you and me
What can I say he lives his way?
He's cloud nine to you and me

HALF IN HALF

I am part fairy though I have no wings
Yet I do have the sparkle that my mystery brings
I'm not that big, I'm not that tall
I'm the right size for me, for a fairy I'm tall
Every now and again one of God's creatures knocks on my door
Just for a chat so we can understand each other more
Our connection with nature is what keeps us alive
Though I think we have forgotten to look into its eyes
Being part fairy keeping the magic alive
When you look into your dreams I'll be the one to open your eyes

FROGS

I love frogs and they love me
As we go over the mountains and into the streams
Living everyday as happy as could be
I love our life well isn't it a scream
Catching flies and bugs and things
Hopping and swimming and lazing around
On lily pads to sunbathe until we are found
For the birds love us too as a tasty snack
They swallow us whole and not just our legs....
As night starts to fall we croak into the dawn
Nature's symphony crickets and all
When the weather gets cold and things start to freeze
We hide for the winter until the spring
When we wake up the cycle begins
From spawn to tadpoles to little frogs again

FOGGED UP

Through the fog and mist
I was set adrift
Wading through
Things that were new

New in the sense
I had to search to find
Things that seemed hard
Not easily defined

Not easily defined
And for so long blind
Blinded by the mist
That suddenly became a storm

Confessed then confused
And kind of amused

I'm sorry were you laughing?

FIGHT

You fight, you fight you move along
Keep getting pulled back from the dawn
It's dusk again it's always dusk
The metal inside has turned to rust
The parts still moving deep inside
They grunt they groan not part of life
The darkness dwells no moon in sight
Relentless it seems from day to night
You live, you hurt you feel your shame
You twist the knot tight again
Everything must go full circle my friend
Where is the start where is the end?
Your minds tense as your body tries to engage
My fist clenched once more to try again

FEEL

If your dreams are ill at ease
Can you blame it on the bees?

If you don't feel so strong
Can one little frog help you move on?

If you feel that you can't say
Can you say the birds took it away?

If you feel that you can't love
Can you blame it on a dove?

If you feel that you can't feel
Can you say that you're for real?

If you feel that you can't fly
Can a broken wing be the reason why?

If you feel the sun is gone
Can you say it's not yet dawn?

If you feel you're in the dark
Can you blame a flameless spark?

If you feel you want to cry
Can you blame the reason?
Why?

FATE

The purple rain the winters fire
The perfect glow the hearts desire
The shifting sand the changing time
The endless life the truth behind
The words unsaid the deeds undone
The act that changed for everyone
The sun, the moon the stars shine on
The snow that falls melts at dawn
The eyes that see the truth inside
The storm that screams right beside
The distorted view the vision almost gone
The hope inside for everyone
The crooked branches the twisted trees
The thoughts that bring you to your knees
The rhyme that knows the stories song
The rhythm that sways on and on
The life you live the love you give
The twist of fate the final bit

FALLING

You are my falling star
My only wish was for you
You are my falling star
In my heart you're true
You are my falling star
You stood out to me
You are my falling star
Together we are free
You are my falling star
You will never fade
You are my falling star
I caught you on the way
You are my falling star
In your light I'll stay
Just to be where you are
And never fade away

FALLING SOFTLY

Falling softly a tear upon your cheek
Falling softly a bird begins to weep
Falling softly a snow flake to the ground
Falling softly a voice loses its sound
Falling softly a feather in the wind
Falling softly a flower at its end
Falling softly a curl upon your face
Falling softly but never from your grace
Falling softly a duvet full of down
Falling softly for you, my dear my crown

FAITH

I've lost faith within myself what am I to do
I've lost faith in all your words and everything you do
I've lost faith that I can see the goodness deep within
I've lost faith that I can hear your message in the wind
I've lost faith that I can touch because it makes me feel
I've lost faith that my broken heart will ever heal
I've lost faith I've lost your scent somewhere in the stream
I've lost faith because I've put all my faith in you
Now it's time for me to go and find my river blue

ENCHANTED

The enchanted forest of wishes and dreams
Reality and illusion, the lines fade in between
Mystery in the mountains, magic in the streams
The dew coated forests are like something from a dream
Gentle little whispers carried in the breeze
What I see and what I hear are beautiful to me
Natures little secrets will somehow be revealed
So, open your heart, and open your mind
Because you never know along the way
The treasures you might find………..

DUSK IS MY LIGHT

I love dusk so give me my pen and my sword
My pen to release my pain my sword to open it again
So, I can write about how life pierces me
How it teases and seduces me
In the half light I can see it all
I can see where I fall and where I can rise again
I succumb to the influence of my creative side
And it all comes alive and me with it
I am a slave to what it holds and what it promises
It's like a release into another world
I am far away from you now as I want to be
I am so close to something more precious than gold
More perfect than anything I've ever known
I see you now through the half light
I am a shadow of my former self
You will be my sun my moon and my every little star
You will smile your wicked little smile
I will fall at your feet I am yours as you are mine
I am transformed and consumed by your presence
I am what you want me to be, yet I do not compromise
Because my love could never be wrong
Because it makes me feel strong
And as the half light turns to night
I know that I am right

DIFFERENT

Why are you so different?
From all the rest
Because I'm on a unique quest
To follow nothing and no one
My quest will be that I shall rise
To be something of a unique surprise
For the quiet one you thought would never shine
Was the one you missed the fire fly in disguise
Well here I am and here I'll stay
The flicker in the night that will not fade away
When you wonder about what I should be
It's not your wonder it's mine it's me

CLEANSED

Blood and anger I can see it flow
Flowing like a river just let it go

There goes the pressure there goes the pain
Here comes the pleasure let it remain

Like the blood that flowed from the body divine
There goes mine but I'm not dying

I must see it flow because I know it's there
Take it to the edge I don't care

Still a life remains with nothing but remains
Another edge......
Another end......
Another chance......

CARRY YOU

I'd carry you on my back
To wherever you'd want to go
Through the burning flames
Through walls of stone
I'd carry you on my back
To where you want to be
To what you most desire
I would take you higher
I'd carry you with me
To help set you free
I'd carry you with me
So, you cloud just be

CAREFREE

She was a happy little soul just like a bumble bee
Buzzing around in her own little world in her own company
She would sing dance and play everything was a mystery
An adventure in the making where she lived wild and free
Anything was possible whether it was real, or it was not
When she spoke with the animals they understood her NOT
But she always imagined they knew exactly what she said
Especially the frogs and their comical little heads
She was not to be detained by anyone or anything
She would not conform to the rules of how life should be
Because she always figured it's better to be me
There were no limitations there were no endless nights
To her there was only one way to live
And by God she did it right

BEAUTY

Who instilled such beauty in you?
The beauty in your mind
The beauty in your soul
The beauty in your heart
The beauty it controlled
The beauty in your voice
In your favourite song
The beauty that would last
And echo in the dawn
The beauty in your eyes
Because they made me see
Like a whisper in the wind
That brought you back to me
The beauty we would share
The dream that was meant to be
The beauty of our lives
That showered you and me
Like the crescent moon we would sit at ease

BE YOURSELF

I'd love to be a candle
And be peaceful in my way
The only thing to bother me
Would be a draft along the way

It seems I'm never happy
With exactly who I am
Always looking for something better
Still searching for a better plan

If I'm not happy
with who I am today
Then I'll be like a candle in the wind
And just get blown away

Unlike a candle
I cannot be replaced
Because when the candle runs out
There's another to take its place

You see I am irreplaceable
Unique in my own way
So, I must accept who I am
And like myself today

To those out there
Who don't see what they want to see
Take me as you get me
Because you'll find me no other way

Well as for being a candle
I guess I'll leave that for today
I'll have to accept who I am
And try not to get blown away

AUTUMN LEAF

An autumn leaf was falling, falling to the ground
The message in the wind tells me what it saw and what it found
While falling from the tree it saw a shooting star
The leaf thought to itself I wish I shoot that far
But instead here I am falling to the floor
Brought down by wind, soaked by rain and frozen to the ground
My life is now at an end I'm fading as I go
But I've still got one job left to do to feed the ground where I lay
All in all, it's not so bad though I will not return again
I have sacrificed my life, so the tree will continue to live
So, in turn there is part of me that will continue to give

BAD NEWS IN A GOOD WAY

So sorry i have to tell you
I've got bad news for you
The plant you gave me to mind
Didn't make it through
It's now gone to plant heaven
Where it will grow again
So when you look on the bright side
It's still alive my friend

AN UNUSUAL FAIRY

Her hair was of golden buttercups plaited together
Her eyes were pools that only the rarest of fish swam in
Her nose could smell all the scents of the earth in one breath
Her ears could hear beyond the sounds of time
Her arms were magic wands ready to grant a wish or take it away
When she danced her feet were musical notes
Her body was the eternal language of love
She spoke with an eloquent beauty beyond which we could understand
Her personality was as light as it was dark
And she spread her love like gold dust touching all that crossed her path

AN ADVENTURE

I will sweep you off your feet
As you shelter beneath my wings
We will soar into the sky
And discover the reason why
We shall explore things together
That will hopefully last forever
The adventure will go on
As we go from dawn to dusk
As we go from dusk to dawn
Our dreams will fuse as one
Now that you're near
I can taste your every tear
To wipe away your fears
For a feeling that's so dear

ALL THAT MATTERS

As bright as the sun
As dark as the night
As silent as a shadow
As it creeps up behind
As urgent as a storm
As still as the snow
As sharp as the frost
As it chills to the bone
As deep as the ocean
As shallow as a stream
As high as a mountain
As flat as a green
As important to me
As I am to you
As it's all that matters
all that rings true

ALIVE

Like a heart without a beat
When you're dead on your feet
Life goes on in this sweet morning song
The sun dries the dew
That rests upon your face
You come alive again
To speak softly to me
Like a gentle whisper
Sailing in the breeze
I think my heart just missed a beat

A MEMORY

Sitting by the fire on a long winters night
Reading my book my head in full flight
Little animals in the forest wading through the snow
Trying to find a friend they didn't want to let go
I remember feeling I was with them trudging my way along
Even though there were no paths our instinct drove us on
We listened to the sounds that whistled in the breeze
The trees felt like giants and we felt ill at ease
The shadows big and dark the mood so very real
The mystery of the forest never ready to reveal
It's a scene that I remember, and I guess I always will
From the comfort of the fire to the stories icy chill
It's my place where I feel warm it's my place where I feel free
It's my place where I feel secure the way life should be

2:1

One heart beats alone
Wrapped in a cocoon
It seems there's no more room

It was set free
To blow in the breeze
Over open ground
Has yet to be found

Should that breeze become a storm
Leave that heart beaten and torn
Stripped from its cocoon
Left in ruins

How long will it be?
Before that heart can see
That two will make it strong
Beating together as one